Isaac Asimov's
21st Century
Library of the Universe

Past and Present

Space Junk

BY ISAAC ASIMOV
WITH REVISIONS AND UPDATING BY RICHARD HANTULA

Gareth Stevens Publishing
A WORLD ALMANAC EDUCATION GROUP COMPANY

Please visit our web site at: **www.garethstevens.com**
For a free color catalog describing Gareth Stevens Publishing's list of high-quality
books and multimedia programs, call 1-800-542-2595 (USA) or 1-800-387-3178 (Canada).
Gareth Stevens Publishing's fax: (414) 332-3567.

The reproduction rights to all photographs and illustrations in this book are controlled by the individuals
or institutions credited on page 32 and may not be reproduced without their permission.

Library of Congress Cataloging-in-Publication Data available upon request from publisher.
Fax (414) 336-0157 for the attention of the Publishing Records Department.

ISBN 0-8368-3983-8 (lib. bdg.)

This edition first published in 2006 by
Gareth Stevens Publishing
A Member of the WRC Media Family of Companies
330 West Olive Street, Suite 100
Milwaukee, WI 53212 USA

Revised and updated edition © 2006 by Gareth Stevens, Inc. Original edition published in
1989 by Gareth Stevens, Inc. under the title *Space Garbage*. Second edition published in 1995
by Gareth Stevens, Inc. under the title *Pollution in Space*. Text © 2006 by Nightfall, Inc.
End matter and revisions © 2006 by Gareth Stevens, Inc.

Series editor: Mark J. Sachner
Art direction: Tammy West
Cover design: Melissa Valuch
Layout adaptation: Melissa Valuch and Jenni Gaylord
Picture research: Kathy Keller
Additional picture research: Diane Laska-Swanke
Artwork commissioning: Kathy Keller and Laurie Shock
Production director: Jessica Morris
Production coordinator: Robert Kraus

The editors at Gareth Stevens Publishing have selected science author Richard Hantula to bring
this classic series of young people's information books up to date. Richard Hantula has written
and edited books and articles on science and technology for more than two decades. He was
the senior U.S. editor for the *Macmillan Encyclopedia of Science*.

In addition to Hantula's contribution to this most recent edition, the editors would like to
acknowledge the participation of two noted science authors, Greg Walz-Chojnacki and
Francis Reddy, as contributors to earlier editions of this work.

Printed in the United States of America

1 2 3 4 5 6 7 8 9 09 08 07 06 05

Contents

We live in an enormously large place — the Universe. It's only natural that we would want to understand this place, so scientists and engineers have developed instruments and spacecraft that have told us far more about the Universe than we could possibly imagine.

We have seen planets up close, and spacecraft have even landed on some. We have learned about quasars and pulsars, supernovas and colliding galaxies, and black holes and dark matter. We have gathered amazing data about how the Universe may have come into being and how it may end. Nothing could be more astonishing.

We have explored many areas of our Solar System, especially the regions close to Earth. We have sent numerous rockets into space, many of which continue to orbit Earth even after they stop working. The result is that nearby outer space is filled with debris — or space junk. This book takes a look at such pollution in space and shows why scientists are concerned.

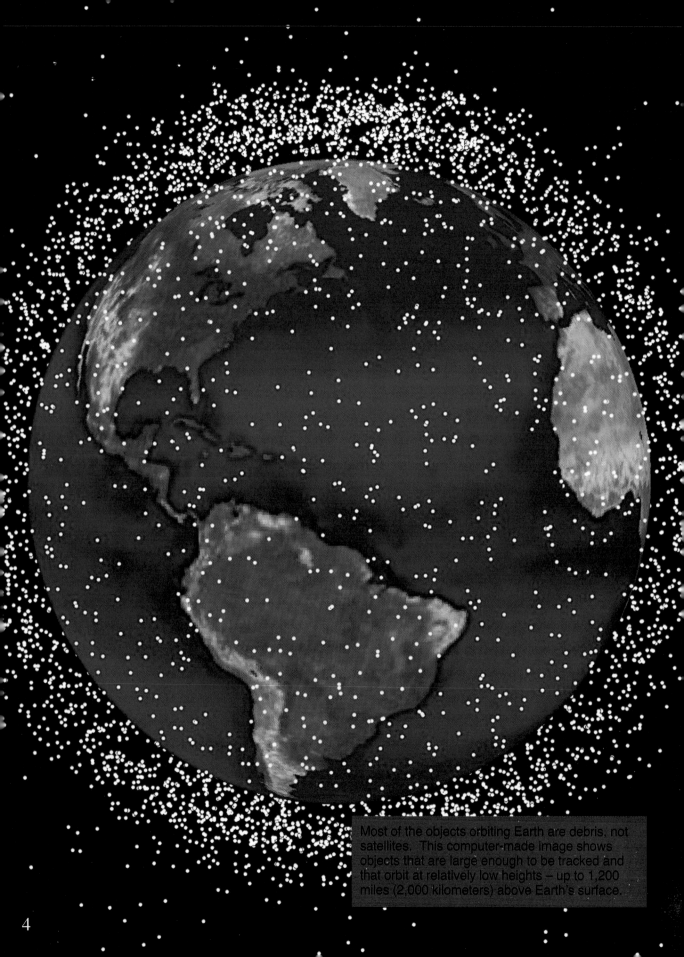

Most of the objects orbiting Earth are debris, not satellites. This computer-made image shows objects that are large enough to be tracked and that orbit at relatively low heights – up to 1,200 miles (2,000 kilometers) above Earth's surface.

4

A Junkyard in Space

Satellites have been placed in orbit around Earth since the late 1950s. Many of these satellites are still circling our planet, even if they are no longer working. Some old satellites have broken apart. There are also bits of rockets that stayed in space after their original jobs were completed. Other types of things put by humans in space range from items left by astronauts, to tiny chips of paint, to debris from weapon tests.

While some space junk drops into the lower atmosphere and either is destroyed or falls to the ground, much remains in orbit for a long, long time. As a result, there are now more than 100,000 pieces of space debris at least the size of a sugar cube estimated to be circling Earth. The number of pieces of smaller size is probably in the millions.

Fortunately, there is a lot of room in space. But as more and more satellites and other spacecraft are put into orbit, the problem of space junk gets bigger.

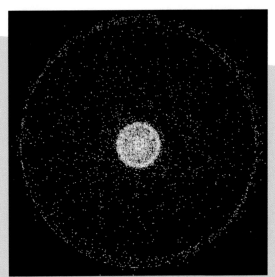

Right: This computer-produced image is made from space high above the North Pole. From this vantage point it is easy to see that many of the objects are concentrated in low orbits or in the "geosynchronous region" about 22,200 miles (35,800 km) above Earth's surface.

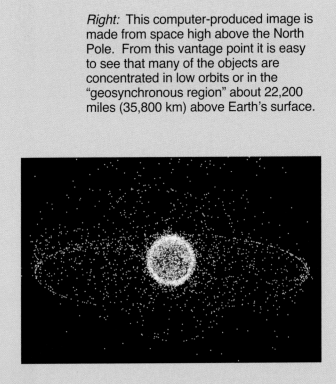

Left: This computer-produced image is made from far enough out in space to be able to see objects in the so-called geosynchronous region about 22,200 miles (35,800 km) above Earth's surface. An object at this height moves at the same rate as Earth rotates, so it is able to stay above more or less the same spot on the surface.

Divide and Multiply

One big problem with space debris is that it can multiply. When a piece of debris breaks apart as a result of a collision with another piece of space junk, its pieces can start colliding with each other. Where there were two objects, soon there are hundreds more!

Another problem is that space debris moves very fast — thousands of miles (kilometers) per hour — and with great force. In space, a piece of aluminum the size of a sugar cube can hit with the force of a 60-pound (27-kilogram) safe moving at 60 miles (100 km) an hour!

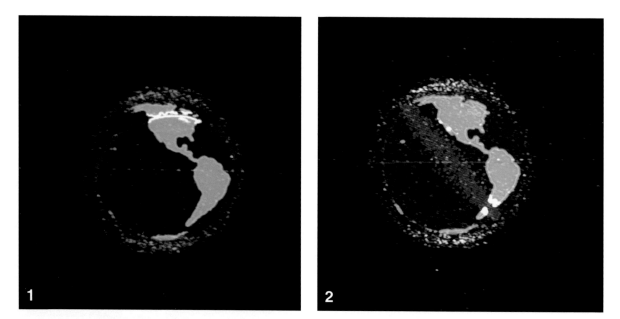

Above and opposite: Scientists studying the debris orbiting Earth used a computer to show how a piece of space junk gradually turns into a cloud of dangerous debris.

Lunar litter — the last trace of humanity?

Suppose that a nuclear war wipes out all of humanity. Gradually, wind, water, and any remaining forms of life then destroy what is left of our cities. If visitors from some other civilization come to Earth millions of years later, they may find no sign that humans ever existed. But on the Moon, where wind, water, and life are absent, the story would be different. The litter that U.S. astronauts left behind on their visits between 1969 and 1972 would still be there, looking almost as it did originally.

If we let pollution in space get out of control, we'll end up with a space environment where there are constant collisions creating ever more debris — and then more collisions!

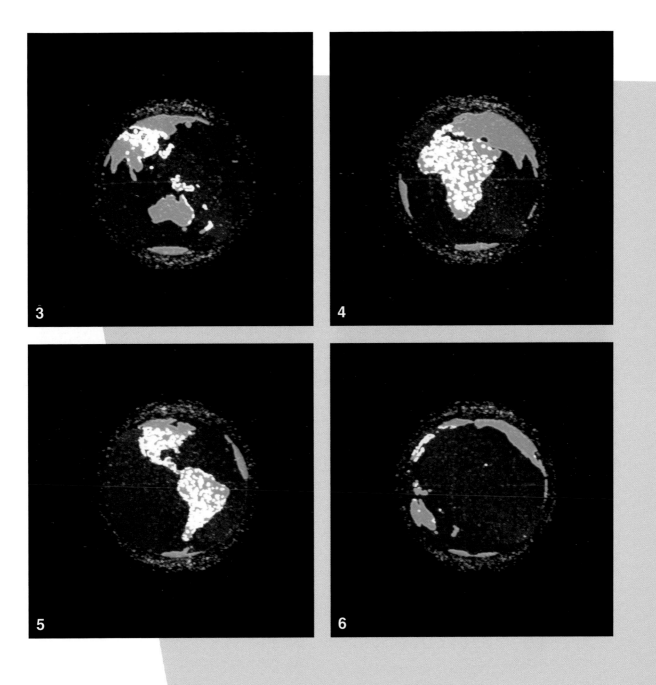

Running Out of Outer Space

Space junk is a problem not just because it's messy. It also can be dangerous. If we send additional satellites into space, we don't want to put them into an orbit where they will collide with a piece of debris and be destroyed.

It is important to know where space junk is — especially the big pieces, which are more dangerous. Radar is one of the ways used to keep track of larger objects in space. Radar uses radio waves, which bounce off satellites and debris, giving scientists on Earth the exact location of each object (whether working or dead) along with an indication of where it is headed. This helps determine a good orbit for the next satellite.

But one day we just may run out of safe orbits!

Left: The U.S. Space Control Center under Cheyenne Mountain in Colorado keeps track of larger pieces of space debris — well over 9,000 items as of the end of 2004.

Right: For several nights following the launch of *Skylab* in 1973, several "extra" satellites streaked across the night sky. They were parts of the rocket that launched the space laboratory.

Radar dishes such as these are part of a worldwide electronic "trash-tracking" network designed to locate debris in outer space.

Above: A flake of paint made a tiny crater *(inset)* in the windshield of the U.S. space shuttle *Challenger*.

Above: Many tiny craters like this (in a magnified view) were found on the *Solar Maximum* satellite after its return to Earth in 1984. High-speed flakes of paint did the damage.

Tiny, but Deadly, Dangers

Space contains numerous meteoroids, most of which are the size of a grain of sand. But they move at many miles (km) a second, and even a small one can puncture a space suit and kill an astronaut. Luckily, space is vast, and so far no "killer meteoroid" has struck an astronaut.

Space debris is equally dangerous. A flake of paint struck a space shuttle in 1983 and chipped the windshield, which had to be replaced at a cost of $50,000. A slightly larger object might have punctured the windshield and caused the deaths of the astronauts on board.

After the space shuttle *Columbia* was destroyed in the atmosphere in 2003, experts looked hard for the cause. At first, many experts suspected the disaster was due to a collision with space debris. Eventually a piece of foam insulation that damaged the craft's wing during launch was blamed. In either case, the accident showed how easy it is to seriously damage a spacecraft.

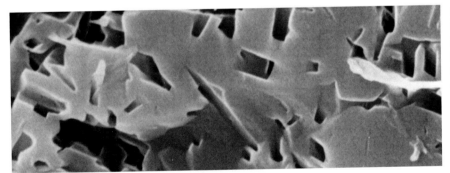

Left: Particles streaming from the Sun leave their marks (magnified) on Moon rocks. However, Earth's atmosphere deflects most of these particles.

Solar wind – another kind of debris

The Sun is constantly hurling out "debris"– electrically charged particles called the solar wind. This radiation can be harmful but usually is not strong enough to threaten astronauts' lives. However, occasionally there is an explosion on the Sun called a solar flare. Then the number of particles rises to a deadly level. An enormous solar flare took place in 1972 during an interval between two missions to the Moon. Fortunately, no astronauts were in space at the time.

The *International Space Station*, as it looked in 2001. The large station, whose assembly began in 1998, is a joint project of the United States, Russia, Japan, the European Space Agency, and Canada.

The Space Station — A Big Target

Space debris is a danger for the *International Space Station*, which is a very big target. Assembly of the space station began in 1998, and the first crew came on board in 2000. Construction was expected to take years, but by 2002 the station already was quite large, measuring 146 feet (44.5 m) long, 240 feet (73 m) wide, and 90 feet (27.5 m) high.

Because of the risk of collision with debris, key areas of the space station are protected with special shielding. The *International Space Station* is the most heavily shielded spacecraft ever. The shielding can keep tiny pieces of debris from penetrating. It cannot stop a fast-moving large piece, but such debris occurs rarely. Also, if a large piece were observed to be approaching, the crew might have enough time to move the space station out of the way. In addition, the *International Space Station* has airtight compartments. If one compartment is punctured, the crew can seal it off and go to other, safer quarters.

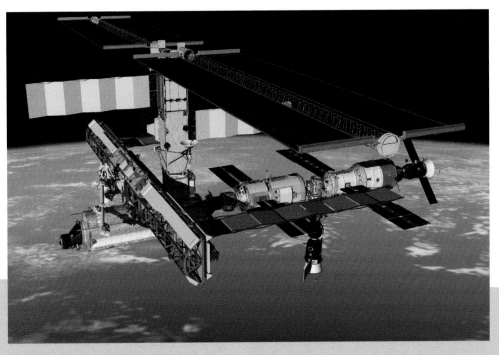

Above: The *International Space Station*'s compartments can be sealed off from one another. If one compartment is damaged, astronauts can move to another for safety.

Hurricane Juan was tracked by a weather-watching satellite *(inset)*.

Satellites – Can't Live Without Them

Satellites were first launched into space in the 1950s. Since then the human race has come to depend on information they send back to Earth. For instance, some satellites help predict the weather and track storms.

In addition, some satellites make it possible for people to send messages across the oceans. Other satellites allow sailors to know the exact location of their ships at all times. Still other satellites make it possible for scientists to study Earth – its soil, its oceans, and its crops. And some satellites carry special telescopes and other instruments that astronomers use to explore the Universe. Also important are spy satellites, which provide information for national defense.

We have come to depend on satellites. But as long as we continue to use them, we will continue to have space debris.

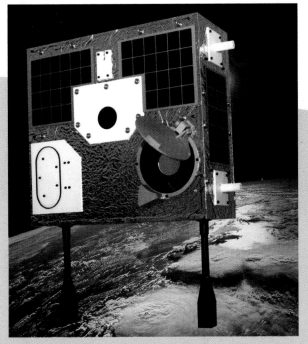

Above: Canada's MOST space telescope, launched in 2003, detects tiny changes in stars' light that cannot be seen from Earth. Its name is short for "Microvariability and Oscillations of STars."

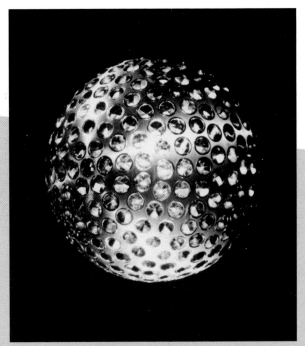

Above: This orbiting "crystal ball" is one of two satellites called *LAGEOS* (Laser Geodynamic Satellite). Laser beams bounced off hundreds of reflectors measure movements in Earth's crust and other characteristics of Earth.

The Sky Is Falling!

Space junk can even be dangerous to living things on Earth. Unless the junk is very high up, debris orbiting Earth encounters thin wisps of Earth's upper air that may gradually slow it down, causing it to come closer to Earth. When small pieces enter the main atmosphere, they just burn up. But large pieces can reach Earth's surface. Nearly three-quarters of these pieces will splash into the ocean, but some may hit land.

In 1978, for example, northern Canada was hit by parts of *Cosmos 954*, a satellite from the former Soviet Union that used radioactive fuel. Also in 1978, increased activity on the surface of the Sun heated Earth's atmosphere, causing it to expand. This increased the atmosphere's "drag" on the U.S. *Skylab* space station, until parts of *Skylab* finally came down in western Australia the following year.

It's not very likely that pieces of satellites will hit buildings or people because most of Earth's surface is covered with water, and much of the rest is territory where few people live. But it is still possible that someday a lump of debris may do some damage.

Left: When the satellite *Cosmos 954* fell to Earth, it scattered radioactive debris that had to be located and safely removed.

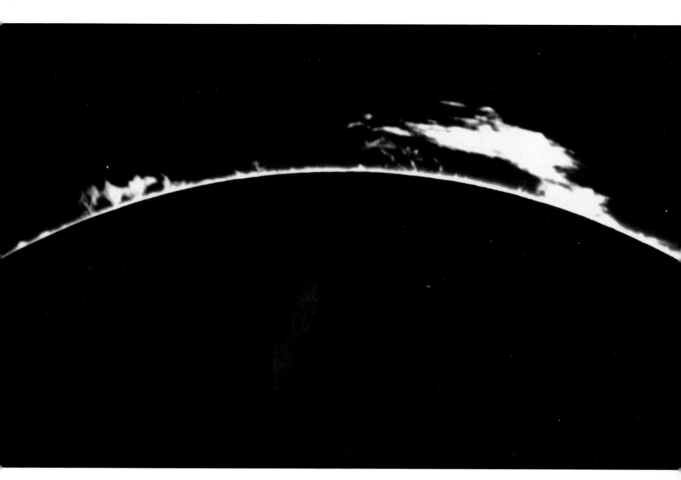

Above: A plume of gas rises above the Sun's surface. This kind of
activity can expand Earth's atmosphere and drag satellites into lower orbits.

Right: Pictured is part
of a water tank
recovered after
Skylab broke apart
in Earth's atmosphere.

What Are the Chances?

About 30 percent of Earth's surface is land, and only about 3 percent of this land has large concentrations of people on it. So if a large piece of debris falls to Earth, the chances are only about 1 in 111 that it might strike land where it might do serious harm to human beings. This means that if a large piece of space debris falls to Earth only once every ten years, then the odds are that it may take a thousand years or more before a piece falls in a place where it could do serious harm to people. Also, even if it fell into a big city, it might hit a spot that happens to be empty.

Of course, by sheer bad luck, a piece of space junk might hit somebody next year. As Earth's population increases daily and cities spread outward, the chances for harm also increase. On the other hand, if we work hard at cleaning up outer space, the chances for harm will decrease.

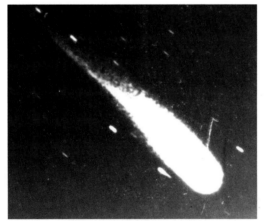

Left: Satellites that fall to Earth burn and break apart in Earth's atmosphere.

Solar flares — life-and-death questions remain

Explosions on the Sun that throw out a deadly flood of charged particles take place at odd times. Scientists don't always know what causes these solar flares or when they'll take place. This means astronauts working at a space station will never know when to expect these dangerous events — so the station has to be shielded at all times. After further study, flares may someday become predictable, and life in space will be safer.

The *Skylab Orbiting Workshop* was launched by the United States in 1973. Pieces of it fell to Earth in 1979.

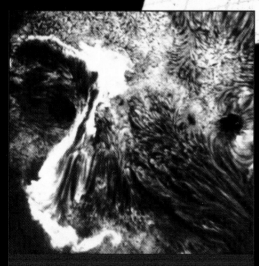

The bright plume of a solar flare leaps above the Sun's surface.

Above: An artist's idea of Mars several centuries from now. Half-buried, and showing signs of erosion, is one of the *Viking* landers, which touched down there in 1976.

Right: An artist's view of one of the two NASA rover vehicles that began exploring the Martian surface in 2004.

To Be or Not to Be? – Space Junk

Much of the debris in nearby outer space will return harmlessly to Earth. In this way, nearby space could be called "self-cleaning." Farther from Earth, space also cleans up after itself much of the time. The probes that have landed on Venus are exposed to high temperatures and strong winds, and they will eventually turn to dust. On Mars, sandstorms might do the same to the remains of probes from Earth, only they will act more slowly.

But on places like our Moon and Phobos (a moon of Mars), there is little or no atmosphere to wear down any litter. On these worlds, debris left behind could last for millions of years. So it is important to remember that under some conditions, our junk may be around forever.

Of course, if we set up a permanent lunar base, we can try to at least keep the Moon clean. But what about the other litter we leave in the cosmos? It will all add up!

Above: One of the landers in the *Venera* series of spacecraft sent by the former Soviet Union to Venus. The probe stopped transmitting about an hour after it landed on the planet's surface – its electronics were destroyed by the tremendous heat there.

Cosmic rays – debris of a dying star?

Cosmic rays are high-speed particles from outer space. They are very energetic and potentially harmful, but usually there are not enough of them to be dangerous. Some come from the Sun, and astronomers think that supernovas are another important source. These violently exploding stars may make the space in their neighborhood deadly for a time. Supernovas occur quite rarely, and only a few stars are close enough to our Solar System to be dangerous! But it's hard to predict when a supernova explosion will take place.

Low orbits are the most littered with space debris. Perhaps one day orbiting "garbage collectors" will be used to clean up these trash-filled orbits.

Preventing and Cleaning Up Space Junk

If too much debris accumulates around Earth, it could become impossible to find safe orbits for future satellites – which might put an end to space exploration.

To help avoid this, countries with major space programs have in recent years tried to design and operate satellites and other spacecraft in ways that tend to keep the production of space junk at a minimum. Engineers have worked on making spacecraft less likely to break apart and better able to survive debris impacts.

Another approach is to remove dead satellites from orbit, although this can be difficult or expensive, depending on the situation. Sometimes satellites whose life is up are steered into the atmosphere, where they are destroyed. In some cases dying satellites are moved into out-of-the-way "graveyard" orbits, where they can't collide with active satellites. One of the tasks of some space shuttle missions has been to pick up satellites that aren't working and repair them or remove them from space.

In the future there may even be a way to sweep up the debris, using lasers or some other powerful technology.

Above: Radar installations at Tyngsborough, Massachusetts, used by NASA to collect data on orbital debris.

On an Endless Journey

Sputnik 1, Earth's first artificial satellite, was put into orbit in 1957. Since then, at least four U.S. space probes launched in the 1970s have gone beyond the known planets: *Pioneer 10*, *Pioneer 11*, *Voyager 1*, and *Voyager 2*. The two *Pioneer* spacecraft no longer have enough power to run their instruments and contact Earth. The two *Voyager* craft are still sending science data back to Earth, but their power supply is expected to be used up by around 2020. After that they, like the *Pioneer* probes will continue moving outward as far-flung pieces of junk.

Other probes will follow, and one day there might be large numbers of such dead objects sailing through interstellar space for countless millions of years. Of what value will these objects be during their endless journey into the cosmos?

Opposite: Earth's deep-space probes sail beyond the known planets of our Solar System. This artist's conception shows *Voyager 2 (foreground)*, with *Pioneers 10 and 11* off to the right. Also shown *(background)* is the path of *Voyager 1*, which passed through the plane of Saturn's rings at a steep angle and headed up and away from the Solar System.

Wandering in interstellar space

As they leave our Solar System, deep-space probes will enter a vastly emptier region. The distances between stars in interstellar space are huge. Astronomers calculate, for example, that *Voyager 2* in about forty thousand years will skim by a red dwarf star named Ross 248. The probe will miss the star by 1.65 light-years. That's almost 10 trillion miles (16 trillion km) – not very close! But it's the closest *Voyager 2* will come to any star other than our Sun in the first million years of its journey.

The "Strange" Planet Earth

A few probes carry with them plaques giving information about Earth and its location. Some carry audio recordings with various sounds on them, including music and the voices of humans speaking. The idea behind this is that someday – perhaps millions of years from now – intelligent beings from other worlds may come across such distant debris and discover the plaques and recordings.

Will it be dangerous to attract the attention of aliens? Probably not; there's no reason to think that intelligent beings from distant planets would be unfriendly.

The plaques and recordings may perhaps even be discovered millions of years from now by human beings living in distant space. Will those humans be able to understand the information sent out such a long time before? Or will they be so distant from Earth in time and space that they will wonder how beings so much like them could have lived on such a "strange" planet like Earth?

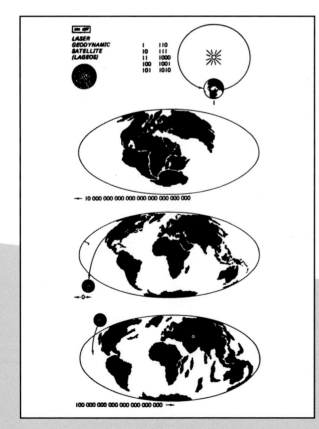

Left: The artificial satellite *LAGEOS 1* (see photo, page 15) is expected to remain in orbit for millions of years. A plaque on board has three maps of Earth's surface, showing the shifting continents over time: one for 268 million years ago, one for the present, and one for 8 million years in the future.

Below: Both *Pioneer 10* and *Pioneer 11* carry a plaque with images of a man and a woman. The man's hand is raised in a sign of goodwill. The plaque also has a diagram of the Solar System showing the probe leaving Earth and sailing into interstellar space.

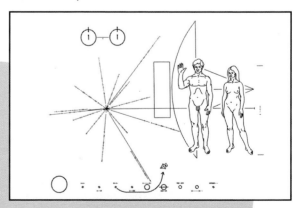

The time is 100 million years from now. The place is somewhere in interstellar space. *Voyager 2* is now just a nonworking craft floating in space in the area of a red supergiant star. The craft is covered with tiny craters caused by the impact of countless meteoroids.

Fact File: Space Junk — Good and Bad

Like many other things, much of what we send into space — or what comes our way from space — can be good or bad. Artificial satellites can help warn us about dangerous storms, but they can also be dangerous themselves when their debris falls to Earth. In the same way, natural objects in space, such as meteoroids, can cause damage on Earth if they fall in the wrong place. But they can also help scientists learn more about the Universe. Listed below are some benefits and drawbacks of various things in space that might be regarded as "junk" or "pollution."

Type of "Space Pollution"	Good Points	Bad Points
Meteoroids and asteroids	May contain substances that help us learn more about the Universe and the origin of life as we know it	May be dangerous if they hit Earth's surface or piloted spacecraft
Piloted spacecraft	Enable humans to explore space firsthand, repair satellites, or return them to Earth if in danger of falling; first step to human colonies in space	Space travel still extremely expensive and dangerous; larger craft orbiting Earth, like *Skylab*, can be dangerous when they fall out of orbit
Satellites	Vital for purposes of navigation, modern communication, weather forecasting, national defense, and space exploration	Expensive; can malfunction; growing number of satellites increases problems and dangers of debris in space
Solar wind and solar flares	Possible future source of energy for Earth and for propelling future spacecraft	Danger to space travelers; danger to humans on Earth if damage to atmosphere continues; disruptive to Earth communications
Unpiloted space probes (Hubble Space Telescope, *Pioneer*, *Voyager*, *Venera*, *Mars Express*, *Cassini*, etc.)	Safe way of exploring and learning about the Universe; can go places no human can safely go, such as the surface of Venus and the outer Solar System and beyond; can help scientists learn things about space they could not learn from a base on Earth	Individual probes can be expensive and take a long time to develop; debris from launch rockets can cause pollution in space; probes take a long time to travel to their destination and begin the transmission of data

Artists' depictions of various objects that may lead to pollution in space: satellites intercept nuclear warheads *(above)*; spacecraft sail through space powered by the Sun *(opposite)*; a meteoroid hits Earth's atmosphere *(below)*; workers in outer space mine the asteroids *(left)*.

More Books about Space Junk

Artificial Satellites. Ray Spangenburg and Kit Moser (Franklin Watts)

Asteroids. Isaac Asimov (Gareth Stevens)

Comets and Meteors. Isaac Asimov (Gareth Stevens)

Man in Space: An Illustrated History from Sputnik to the Shuttle Columbia. Time Magazine (Time Inc. Home Entertainment)

Skylab: The Story of Man's First Station in Space. William J. Cromie (Random House)

Space Exploration Reference Library. Rob Nagel and Peggy Saari (Thomson Gale)

Space Stations. James Barter (Lucent)

Voyager's Grand Tour: To the Outer Planets and Beyond. Henry C. Dethloff and Ronald A. Schorn (Smithsonian)

DVDs

Starry Night: Comet Hunters/Asteroid Seekers. (Imaginova)

Starry Night: Danger! Solar Storm. (Imaginova)

Web Sites

The Internet sites listed here can help you learn about space junk.

European Space Agency. www.esoc.esa.de/external/mso/debris.html
NASA. sn-callisto.jsc.nasa.gov/
Space.com. www.space.com/spacewatch/space_junk.html
United Nations Earthwatch. earthwatch.unep.net/solidwaste/spacejunk.php
Windows to the Universe. www.windows.ucar.edu/tour/link=/games/junk_intro.html

Places to Visit

You can explore outer space — including the places close to our planet where space debris is a problem — without leaving Earth. Here are some museums and centers where you can find a variety of space exploration exhibits and activities.

Canada Science and Technology Museum
1867 St Laurent Blvd
Ottawa, Ontario K1G 5A3
Canada

H.R. MacMillan Space Centre
1100 Chestnut Street
Vancouver, British Columbia V6J 3J9
Canada

Kansas Cosmosphere and Space Center
1100 N. Plum
Hutchinson, Kansas 67501

National Air and Space Museum
Smithsonian Institution
6th and Independence Avenue SW
Washington, DC 20560

Space Center Houston
1601 NASA Road 1
Houston, Texas 77058

U.S. Space and Rocket Center
One Tranquility Base
Huntsville, Alabama 35805

Glossary

atmosphere: the gases that surround a planet, star, or moon.

cosmic rays: fast-moving particles of matter from outer space. Some cosmic rays are produced by the Sun, but many come from beyond the Solar System. Astronomers suspect that some are connected with supernovas.

erosion: the wearing away of an object or substance by such forces as wind, water, or ice.

European Space Agency (ESA): an organization founded in 1975, pooling the resources of several European countries and Canada for joint research and exploration of space.

graveyard orbit: an out-of-the-way orbit where artificial satellites that are no longer useful may be placed so that they do not interfere with working satellites.

interstellar: between or among the stars.

light-year: the distance that light travels in one year — nearly 6 trillion miles (9.6 trillion km).

meteoroid: a lump of rock or metal drifting through space. Meteoroids can be as big as asteroids or as small as specks of dust.

NASA: the space agency in the United States — the National Aeronautics and Space Administration.

orbit: the path that a body follows as it circles, or revolves around, another.

***Pioneer 10* and *11* and *Voyager 1* and *2*:** probes heading beyond the farthest reaches of our Solar System.

planet: a large celestial body that revolves around our Sun or some other star and that is not itself a star.

pollution: the dirtying of the air, land, water, or space.

probe: a craft that travels in space, photographing and studying celestial bodies and in some cases even landing on them.

radio waves: electromagnetic waves that can be detected by radio-receiving equipment.

red dwarf star: a cool, faint star, smaller than our Sun. Red dwarfs are probably the most numerous stars in our Galaxy, but are so faint they are very hard to see.

satellite: a smaller body that orbits a larger body. *Sputnik 1* was Earth's first artificial satellite. The Moon is Earth's natural satellite.

Skylab: a U.S. space station launched in 1973. Three separate crews lived and worked in it in 1973-1974. It fell to Earth in 1979.

solar flare: a huge explosion of intensely heated gases on the Sun that hurls out great energy. Flares occur near sunspots, the cooler, darker areas of the Sun.

Solar System: the Sun with the planets and all the other bodies, such as asteroids and comets, that orbit it.

solar wind: tiny particles that travel from the Sun's surface at speeds of hundreds of miles a second.

space shuttle: a mostly reusable space craft launched into space by a rocket but capable of returning to Earth under its own power. The first space shuttle, *Columbia*, was launched in 1981 by the United States.

space station: a large artificial satellite with enough room for people to live and work for long periods of time.

supernova: the explosive collapse of a very large star. When a supernova occurs, material from the star is spread through space.

Index

Born in 1920, Isaac Asimov came to the United States as a young boy from his native Russia. As a young man, he was a student of biochemistry. In time, he became one of the most productive writers the world has ever known. His books cover a spectrum of topics, including science, history, language theory, fantasy, and science fiction. His brilliant imagination gained him the respect and admiration of adults and children alike. Sadly, Isaac Asimov died shortly after the publication of the first edition of *Isaac Asimov's Library of the Universe*.

The publishers wish to thank the following for permission to reproduce copyright material: front cover, 3, 27, © Adolph Schaller 1988; 4, 5 (both), 10 (upper, inset), 10 (lower), 11, 13, 14 (both), 15 (right), 17 (lower), 19 (large), 23, 26 (both), 29 (lower left), NASA; 6-7 (all), Courtesy of Spacecraft Engineering Department, Naval Research Laboratory; 8 (left), 18, Courtesy of United States Space Command; 8 (right), © Dennis Milon; 9, Courtesy of COMSAT; 10 (upper, large), Courtesy of Rockwell International; 12, NASA Marshall Space Flight Center; 15 (left), European Space Agency; 16, Courtesy of United States Department of Energy; 17 (upper), © Jon Pons/Courtesy of Del Woods of DayStar Filter Corporation; 19 (inset), National Optical Astronomy Observatories; 20 (upper), © Bruce Bond; 20 (lower), Jet Propulsion Laboratory; 21, © David A. Hardy; 22, © Pat Rawlings 1988; 25, © Julian Baum 1988; 28, © Rick Sternbach; 29 (upper), Los Alamos National Laboratory; 29 (lower right), © Mark Maxwell 1985.